GEORGE GROSZ

THE DAY OF RECKONING

GEORGE GROSZ

THE DAY OF RECKONING

Introduction and notes
by FRANK WHITFORD

Allison & Busby
LONDON · NEW YORK

Abrechnung folgt!
first published 1925 by Malik Verlag, Berlin.
This edition published 1984
by Allison & Busby Ltd,
6a Noel Street, London W1V 3RB
and distributed in the USA by
Schocken Books Inc.,
200 Madison Avenue, New York, NY 10016

British Library Cataloguing in Publication Data

Grosz, George
    The day of reckoning.
    1. Grosz, George   2. Germany in art
    I. Title II. Whitford, Frank III. Abrechnung folgt. *English*
    741.943   NC251.G66

    ISBN 0–85031–515–8

Set in Helvetica by
Falcon Graphic Art Ltd.,
Wallington, Surrey
Printed and bound in Great Britain by
Richard Clay (The Chaucer Press)
Bungay, Suffolk

Contents

Introduction

The Day of Reckoning was published in 1923 and is so similar to *The Face of the Ruling Class*, which appeared two years earlier, that it might be regarded as the second volume of the same work. Both consist of political cartoons attacking the politicians, the military and the social parasites, and advertising the plight of the working poor. Both books were published by the *Malik Verlag* and most of the drawings reproduced in both had already appeared elsewhere.

The *Malik Verlag* was a publishing house formed in 1916 by Wieland Herzfelde, a writer of revolutionary political views who at that time was only twenty years of age. Herzfelde was eventually to bring out a series of political and satirical magazines (like *Everyman his own Football*, *Bankruptcy*, *The Truncheon* and *Deadly Earnest*) and books with a strong social and political message. He published novels by Upton Sinclair, for example, and John Reed's *Ten Days that Shook the World*.

Herzfelde was not only responsible for bringing Grosz's work to public attention. He also encouraged the artist to become a political cartoonist and gave Grosz's emotional and often vague opinions a clear direction. For about ten years Grosz worked for almost no one else. The *Malik Verlag* published portfolios of his prints, his cartoons and even his poetry. Grosz was even involved in the editing of some of the magazines.

Herzfelde and Grosz met in a way that speaks volumes about the personality of both. They were introduced in 1915 at a party given by the eccentric expressionist painter Ludwig Meidner in his Berlin flat. Grosz was 22 and Herzfelde scarcely out of school. Most of those present were pacifists, republicans or both and Grosz, always fond of pretending to be someone else, introduced himself as a Dutch entrepreneur (Holland was neutral in the Great War) quietly making a fortune from the sale, as ashtrays or other souvenirs suitably inscribed with jingoistic slogans, of shrapnel, empty shell cases, or the steel helmets of dead soldiers.

Grosz, by then as opposed to the war as anyone present, had nicely calculated the effect of his charade on Meidner's earnest, humourless guests. Once the outrage had subsided, Grosz revealed his true identity. Once Herzfelde had seen his work, he proposed a collaboration.

Grosz also became a friend of Herzfelde's older brother Helmut who, as a protest against the Kaiser's regularly repeated prayer that God should 'punish England', had anglicised his name to John Heartfield. Heartfield was an artist, too, and worked closely with Grosz. They refined the new technique of photomontage (which they claimed to have invented) and employed it as a political weapon. Heartfield, discouraged by Grosz's apparently limitless skill with pen and pencil, abandoned drawing and devoted himself to photomontage which, in his hands, became an incomparable propagandist tool, especially after the Nazis came to power.

Censorship and other forms of official interference prevented the *Malik Verlag* from expressing its revolutionary political message with any vehemence until the war was over. After 1918, and in spite of continuing governmental opposition, Herzfelde and his collaborators repeatedly declared their support for the Communists and their opposition to the regime. Many of their magazines were banned as soon as they appeared; Herzfelde and his associates were brought to trial for libel, making the military appear ridiculous and even for blasphemy.

1919 and 1920 were years in which Grosz produced many of his most memorable drawings and many of them were subsequently reproduced in anthologies like *The Day of Reckoning*. 1920 was a crucial year for Grosz, both as a man and as an artist. He married; he had his first exhibition of paintings (at a private art gallery in Munich); and in the same year he demonstrated that such concessions to bourgeois conventions were, as yet, nothing more than straws in the gentlest of winds. In 1920 he also wrote some of his most trenchant, (Marxist) art criticism and helped organise the 'First international Dada fair' in Berlin, an exhibition of paintings, objects and slogans, most of which were intended to annoy the public and condemn the government and the military. That they were successful in this was proved by the authorities' decision to close the exhibition down.

The Face of the Ruling Class was published in 1921 and in the following year Grosz's political allegiance was subjected to severe strain. In 1922 he travelled to the Soviet Union for the first time and stayed there for six months, working on a book with the Danish author Martin Andersen-Nexö. It was then that he came face to face with conditions in the world's first workers' state and measured the gulf between the propagandists' image and reality.

Grosz was disillusioned even by Lenin whom he briefly met and who reminded him of a provincial pharmacist. He quickly came to the conclusion that the awesome privation had been made worse by arrogant bureaucracy and rigid adherence to party dogma. Was this the utopia which he and his friends were labouring to build in Germany?

For some time Grosz kept his doubts private and almost nothing of his growing scepticism emerged in his work for several years. The certainty of the message proclaimed by *The Face of the Ruling Class* also rings out from *The Day of Reckoning* and from *Ecce Homo*, which is even more brilliant and bitter. We must remember however, that although the last two of these anthologies were published after Grosz's return from the Soviet Union, they consist almost entirely of
ix   drawings produced some time before.

Nevertheless, with the benefit of hindsight we can perceive in *The Day of Reckoning* the hesitant beginnings of an approach that would eventually dominate Grosz's art, the first faint signs of a development in which the political cartoonist would become a benign social reporter. In a very small number of the drawings there is a hint of sympathy with subjects which previously had been bitterly attacked. Look, for example, at No.57 which shows an engagement between a young girl and a crabbed old man. The participants appear ugly, repulsive and even devious, but they have been drawn with a feeling not only for themselves as individuals, but also for the entire milieu to which they belong.

Grosz's secret sympathy with subjects which he attacks is matched by his lack of understanding with the ostensible heroes of his drawings. Time and time again workers are shown as mere ciphers (see, for example, Nos.56 and 59). Significantly, too, the same workers' faces appear repeatedly in different drawings, a sure sign of a failure of imagination, of an ability to identify with the subject.

Some of Grosz's contemporaries, not least writers in the Communist press, noticed and commented upon this contradictory attitude to the heroes and villains in the drawings. In his preface to the early drama *Drums in the Night*, Bert Brecht surmises that Grosz one day must have discovered within himself 'a powerful and irresistible love for a particular and typical kind of face' which just happened to be the same as 'the face of the ruling class'. It was love and not hatred therefore, which inspired Grosz in his choice and use of his subjects. The political conviction was almost an afterthought.

Grosz's political views were never entirely clear, especially to himself: the sharp focus would never have been achieved without the help of Wieland Herzfelde. The accuracy of Brecht's insight was in any case confirmed by subsequent events. The political purpose of Grosz's art was gradually replaced by the desire to record, without comment, the world of the German bourgeois which gradually became the world in which Grosz felt most at home. Soon after emigrating to the United States early in 1933 he enrolled his sons in private schools and put down their names for Harvard University.

Frank Whitford

THE DAY OF RECKONING

3   Black white and red unto death

4   What are reparation debts – I'm not having my seat pulled out from under my arse!

5   'Poverty is a great inner radiance' (Rilke)

6   Keep at it

7   Although he got sick in the Ruhr, things don't taste bad

8   The Republic sits fast and snores

9   'Sporting club Harmonia'

10   MARLOH NOW – what a crusading knight of the Swastika wants to be …

11   – AND BEFORE … practised betimes

12   Swim, he who can, and whoever is too weak, go under

13　The day of reckoning is coming

14   Traitors

15 Love the Fatherland, be quiet

16   My pension …

17 Equals one Havana

18 Song of the intellectuals:
Take my body, possessions, honour, child and wife,
but my mind must remain my own!

19 People of Europe, protect your holiest possessions

20 The rich get the booty – the people the privations of war

21   In spite of hunger and shame we shall never be forced to bend the knee!

22 The bourgeois baits …

23   … and the proletarian has to bleed

24   We want to beat France. …

25   Against Communism they are united!

26 The family is the foundation of the State

27   Half a century of Social Democracy

28 Careful, do not trip!

29 A beloved wife, a charming child,
    That is my heaven on earth

30   United front

31 Religion must be preserved for the people!

33 Tie yourself to the Fatherland, dear Fatherland!

34   The stage director …

35   … and his puppets

36 The workers cause the authorities so much trouble …

37　… that they find it impossible to catch the profiteers

38   Two chimneys and a single soul

39   Stinnes and his President

40 Be loyal and upright
Into your cool grave

41   Give us this day our daily bread

42   The Republic – a scarecrow

DAS DEUTSCHE KAISERREICH

IST·DIE SEHNSUCHT

UNSRER ZUKUNFT

(HELFFERICH)
IM REICHSTAG 22.VI

Wenn einst der Kaiser kommen wird
Schlagen wir zum Krüppel den Wirth.
Knallen die Gewehre — tack, tack, tack
Aufs schwarze und aufs rote Pack!
(Aus einem Nationalgesang der Reaktionäre.)

ARBEITER! BESTEHT DARAUF,
DASS DIESE GESELLSCHAFT
UNSCHÄDLICH GEMACHT WIRD!!

43   Poster on the assassination of Rathenau

44   He who feeds well …

45   ... easily forgets us

46 The Görlitz Programme …

47   … and its consequences

48 The German philistine is a gut
    Filled with fears and hopes that God will be merciful (Herwegh)

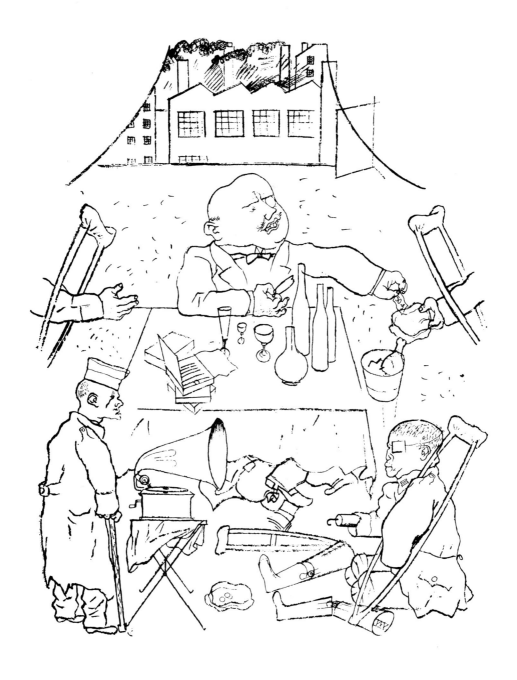

49   … the war-wounded are becoming a veritable national nuisance!

50   One's own home is worth its weight in gold

51   Jews out!

52 The stab in the back from the Right

53   Four years of murder

54   If the soldiers were not such idiots,
     they would have run away from me ages ago (Fridericus Rex)

55 If the workers wish to cease being slaves,
    they have to wrest the knout from their masters

56   Enjoy life!

57 Marriage is the beginning and the summit of culture (Goethe)

58 We are holding together fast and true

59   Damned of this earth, awake!

Notes

3 Black white and red unto death
   Schwarz-weiß-rot bis in den Tod
   These were the colours of the old Imperial
   flag, replaced in the Weimar Republic with
   the black, red and gold which had stood for
   independence and democracy since the
   French occupation during the Napoleonic
   wars. The embittered, middle-aged
   monarchist looks like a petty official or
   schoolteacher.

4 What are reparation debts – I'm not having
   my seat pulled out from under my arse!
   *Was heißt Reparationsschuld – ich werde
   mir doch nicht den Sitz unterm Arsch
   wegziehen lassen!*
   The capitalist sitting on a mound of money
   and share (*Aktie*) certificates, has a diamond
   in his cravat, the ribbon of the Iron Cross in
   his buttonhole and a swastika hanging from
   his watchchain.

5 'Poverty is a great inner radiance' (Rilke)
   'Armut ist ein großer Glanz von innen'

6 Keep at it
   Durchhalten
   The building with the low spire in the
   background is the Kaiser Wilhelm memorial
   church in the wealthy, Western part of Berlin.
   A beggar and a limbless ex-serviceman wait
   in front of a delicatessen while fashionable,
   uninterested people hurry past.

7. Although he got sick in the Ruhr, things don't
   taste bad
   *Obwohl an der Ruhr erkrankt, schmeckt's
   ihm nicht schlecht*
   Although the Ruhr is occupied by foreign

troops, the capitalist continues to live high
on the hog.

8 The Republic sits fast and snores
   Fest sitzt und schnarcht die Republik
   The leaders of the new Germany
   (Scheidemann, Ebert and others) gamble
   while the contented bourgeois sleeps.

9 'Sporting club Harmonia'
   'Sportklub Harmonia'
   A comment on covert rearmament. Since
   Germany was forbidden to rearm, sporting
   clubs encouraged military skills.

10 MARLOH NOW – what a crusading knight
   of the Swastika wants to be …
   *MARLOH JETZT – Was ein Haken-kreuzritter
   werden will …*

11 – AND BEFORE … practised betimes
   – UND EINST … übt sich bei Zeiten
   Marloh was a lieutenant in the *Freikorps* who,
   in 1919, was responsible for the massacre
   of 28 revolutionary sailors in their
   headquarters in Berlin. At his trial, Marloh
   admitted giving the order to execute the men
   and said that he had really wanted to kill 300
   of them. He was acquitted. No.11 shows him
   carrying out the execution. A machine gun
   was actually used. The title includes a pun:
   the German for swastika, the symbol of the
   Nationalists, is *Hakenkreuz*, for crusader,
   Kreuzritter. Marloh is a *Haken-kreuzritter*.

12 Swim, he who can, and whoever is too weak,
   go under
   *Schwimme, wer schwimmen kann, und wer
   zu schwach ist, gehe unter*

13 The day of reckoning is coming!
   Abrechnung folgt!
   Grosz's reaction to the events of March 1919
   when the *Freikorps* put the revolution down.

14 Traitors
   Hochverräter

15 Love the Fatherland, be quiet
Lieb Vaterland, magst ruhig sein
The composition consciously echoes Manet's
'Execution of the Emperor Maximilian' and
Goya's 'The Third of May 1808'.

16 My pension ...
Meine Rente –

17 Equals one Havana
= eine Havana

18 Song of the intellectuals:
Take my body, possessions, honour, child
and wife,
but my mind must remain my own!
Gesang der Intellektuellen:
Nehmen Sie den Leib, Gut, Ehr, Kind und
Weib,
der Geist muß uns doch bleiben!

19 People of Europe, protect your holiest
possessions
Völker Europas, wahrt eure heiligsten Güter
A collection of Grosz's stock types. Clockwise:
a journalist for the Social Democratic paper
Vorwärts (Forward), a whore, a capitalist, a
policeman, a priest and a judge.

20 The rich get the booty –
the people the privations of war
Für die Reichen ist die Beute –
Für das Volk die Not der Kriege

21 In spite of hunger and shame we shall never
be forced to bend the knee!
Trotz Hunger und Schmach, wir lassen uns
nie und nimmer in die Knie zwingen!
Obviously a portrait, but the sitter cannot be
identified.

22 The bourgeois baits ...
Der Bürger hetzt –
Screaming slogans ('My hand is not yet
withered'; 'Give him one'), a pack of
Nationalists attack one of the French
occupying forces.

23 ... and the proletarian has to bleed
– und der Prolet muß bluten
An old man holds up a Nationalist newspaper
with the headline 'Just let them come!' while
a French officer leads a bayonet charge.

24 We want to beat France....
Siegreich wollen wir Frankreich
schlagen.....

25 Against Communism they are united!
Gegen den Kommunismus sind sie einig!
A French and German officer link hands.

26 The family is the foundation of the State
Die Familie ist die Grundlage des Staates

27 Half a century of Social Democracy
Ein halbes Jahrhundert Sozialdemokratie

28 Careful, do not trip!
Vorsicht, nicht stolpern!

29 A beloved wife, a charming child,
That is my heaven on earth
Ein trautes Weib, ein herzig Kind,
Das ist mein Himmel auf der Erde
The woman is singing the carol 'Silent
Night'.

30 United front
Einheitsfront

31 Religion must be preserved for the people!
Die Religion muß dem Volke erhalten
bleiben!
The priest is saying, 'Be fruitful and
multiply'.

32 Knowledge is power
Wissen ist Macht
The text on the blackboard reads: (10% wage
deductions) (United front). The future of the
working people lies in the flowering of
business. (Contract) (12 hour working day).

33 Tie yourself to the Fatherland, dear
Fatherland!
Ans Vaterland, ans teure, schließ dich an!
'Class justice' is written on the whip handle.
One of the share certificates is for Sarotti, a
leading chocolate manufacturer.

34 The stage director ...
Der Regisseur –

35 ... and his puppets
– und seine Puppen

36 The workers cause the authorities so much
trouble ...
*Die Arbeiter machen der Obrigkeit so viel
zu schaffen ...*

37 ... that they find it impossible to catch the
profiteers
*... daß es ihr nicht möglich ist, die Schieber
zu fassen*

38 Two chimneys and a single soul
Zwei Schlote und eine Seele
Hugo Stinnes was one of the leading
capitalists of the period who controlled the
commanding heights of the German economy.
He was also an influential member of
Parliament. Louis Loucheur was his French
equivalent, an industrialist and politician who
had been Minister for Armaments and a
member of the French delegation at
Versailles. In 1921 he became Minister for
Reparations and the 'Liberated Territories'.

39 Stinnes and his President
Stinnes und sein Präsident
The pupplet is Friedrich Ebert, Social
Democrat and first President of the Weimar
Republic.

40 Be loyal and upright
into your cool grave
*Ueb immer Treu und Redlichkeit
Bis in dein kühles Grab*

41 Give us this day our daily bread
Unser täglich Brot gib uns heute

42 The Republic – a scarecrow
Die Republik – ein Spatzenschreck

43 Poster on the assassination of Rathenau
Plakat anläßlich des Mordes an Rathenau
The text reads: THE GERMAN EMPIRE is
the longing of our future (Helfferich) in the
Reichstag 22.VI
If the Kaiser shall one day come
we shall beat Wirth and cripple him
The guns report – bang, bang, bang
on the pack of blacks and reds!
(From a national song of the reactionaries)
WORKERS! Insist that this society is rendered
harmless!!
Karl Helfferich was one of the wildest of the
Nationalists in the German Parliament. In
1918 he had been the German representative
in Moscow. He had also been Minister of
Finance and Vice Chancellor. Josef Wirth had
become German Chancellor in May 1921 and
his policy towards the victorious allies and
their demands for reparations was
considerably more friendly than that of
Helfferich and the Nationalists. Wirth had also
provoked bitter criticism by appointing Walther
Rathenau as Minister for Reconstruction.
Rathenau was an economist, the son of the
founder of the German General Electricity
Company (AEG) and a Jew. In February 1922
he was also appointed Foreign Minister. On
24 June 1922 he was murdered in Berlin by
a group of Nationalists. His assassination
caused an uproar. Helfferich's speech in the
Recihstag, from which the poster quotes,
resulted in his being shouted out of the
debating chamber.

44 He who feeds well ...
Wer gut frißt ...
The toast is to the Kaiser

45 ... easily forgets us
... uns leicht vergißt

46 The Görlitz Programme ...
Das Görlitzer Programm –
In 1921 the Majority Socialists held their party conference in the town of Görlitz. There, moves were made to heal the split in the Socialist Party which had occurred during the war when Karl Liebknecht and his followers had refused to vote for military spending. In 1922 most of the Independent Socialists agreed to rejoin the majority and form the United Social Democratic Party based on the 'Görlitz Programme'. According to the Programme, the Party would now admit bourgeois elements which supported the Republic, the democratisation of the administration and of the military forces. In Grosz's drawing, one of the embracing men seems to be Hugo Stinnes (see No.38). The gramophone is playing 'Dear Fatherland, may you be quiet'. 'Die Glocke' (The bell) was a political journal edited by Parvus, the pseudonym of Alexander Helphand, a maverick Socialist and opponent of Bolshevism.

47 ... and its consequences
– und seine Folgen

48 The German philistine is a gut
Filled with fears and hopes that God will be merciful (Herwegh)
Der deutsche Spießer ist ein Darm,
Gefüllt mit Furcht und Hoffnung, daß Gott erbarm (Herwegh)
George Herwegh was a political poet involved in the revolution of 1848.

49 ... the war-wounded are becoming a veritable national nuisance!
... diese Kriegsverletzten wachsen sich nachgerade zur Landplage aus!
The capitalist is putting a 5-Pfennig note into the beggar's cap.

50 One's own home is worth its weight in gold
Eigner Herd is Goldes Wert

51 Jews out!
Juden raus!

52 The stab in the back from the Right
Der Dolchstoß von rechts
Nationalists believed that Germany had not lost the war, but that it had been 'stabbed in the back' by the Left. Here it is profiteering (*Wucher*) which is doing a miner to death.

53 Four years of murder
Vier Jahre Mord

54 If the soldiers were not such idiots,
they would have run away from me ages ago (Fridericus Rex)
Wenn die Soldaten nicht solche Dummköpfe wären,
würden sie mir schon längst davongelaufen sein (Fridericus Rex)
Frederick the Great, King of Prussia, is regarded as the founder of the Prussian authoritarian state and of the Prussian army.

55 If the workers wish to cease being slaves, they have to wrest the knout from their masters
Wenn die Arbeiter aufhören wollen Sklaven zu sein,
müssen sie ihren Herren die Knute entreißen
The word on the whip handle reads 'class justice' and the capitalist is sitting on money and share certificates.

56 Enjoy life!
Freut Euch des Lebens!

57 Marriage is the beginning and the summit of culture (Goethe)
Die Ehe ist der Anfang und der Gipfel der Kultur (Goethe)
An engagement between a young girl and an old man.

58 We are holding together fast and true
   Wir halten fest und treu zusammen
   Friedrich Ebert (shown by Grosz, as so often,
   as a monarch) with Scheidemann holding on
   to his coat tails, Noske in military uniform and
   Hermann Müller signing the peace treaty.

59 Damned of this earth, awake!
   Wacht auf, Verdammte dieser Erde